SARBANES-OXLEY ONGOING COMPLIANCE GUIDE

D1561994

SARBANES-OXLEY
ONGOING COMPLIANCE
GUIDE

KEY PROCESSES AND SUMMARY CHECKLISTS

ANNE M. MARCHETTI

John Wiley & Sons, Inc.

Library of Congress Cataloging-in-Publication Data

Marchetti, Anne M., 1963-

Sarbanes-Oxley ongoing compliance guide : key processes and summary checklists / Anne M. Marchetti.

p. cm.

Includes index.

ISBN-13: 978-0-471-74686-7 (pbk.)

1. Corporations--Accounting--Law and legislation--United States. 2. Corporations--Auditing--Law and legislation--United States. 3. Financial statements--Law and legislation--United States. 4. Corporations--United States--Accounting. 5. Corporations--United States--Auditing. 6. Financial statements--United States. I. Title.

KF1446.M355 2007

346.73'06648--dc22

2006037549

Printed in the United States of America

10   9   8   7   6   5   4   3   2   1

DEDICATION

To my parents, Jim and Barbara, with thanks for their continuous love and support.

TABLE OF CONTENTS

CHAPTER **3**

THE TIME HAS COME FOR ERM   39

PREFACE

Without dispute, the number-one issue surrounding Sarbanes-Oxley Section 404 compliance is cost. The experience of most organizations is that initial compliance costs grossly exceeded estimates, and the cost of sustaining compliance has been just as burdensome. The expectation that organizations would experience a significant decline in compliance costs subsequent to initial certification has not manifested itself. Most organizations are searching for compliance cost-reduction solutions. My objective for this book is to share with readers vital considerations and components of a detailed ongoing compliance plan, including the use of technology that will assist in reducing ongoing compliance costs, as well as demonstrating how compliance can be utilized to build an effective enterprise risk management program that can assist organizations with strategy execution and achievement of overall objectives. The process checklists and task summaries outlined in the guidebook focus on key areas. It is my hope that they will lead to a more efficient compliance process, ongoing compliance cost reduction, and increased shareholder value.

Anne M. Marchetti

1

THE PATH TO ONGOING COMPLIANCE

THE ORIGINS OF THE SARBANES-OXLEY ACT

A handful of companies have become household names mostly because of their demonstration of corporate greed, fraud, and accounting improprieties. The activities of these few organizations are not representative of the majority of companies in the United States, yet the result of their abuses has left a significant mark on public corporations. Considered the most significant legislation to impact the accounting profession since the Securities Acts of 1933 and 1934, the Sarbanes-Oxley Act of 2002 (the "Act") comprises 11 titles that outline complex compliance requirements affecting a public company's entire organization, including the relationship with its external auditor.

The Act was signed into law to improve the accuracy and transparency of financial reporting and corporate disclosures, as well as to reinforce the importance of corporate ethical standards. In turn, it has placed significant responsibility on issuers to design, implement, and maintain effective systems of internal controls to ensure adequate financial reporting to the Securities and Exchange Commission (SEC) and investors. In addition, the Act imposes significant criminal penalties and fines upon corporate executives who do not comply. Ultimately, the requirements of the Act seek to enhance the quality, accuracy, and timeliness of financial data to allow shareholders to make informed decisions regarding their investments.

GENERATING VALUE FROM COMPLIANCE

The resultant changes from the Sarbanes-Oxley Act, specifically SEC requirements and regulations, have forced businesses to reevaluate their organizational structures and systems of internal control and to create and/or modify the roles of individuals involved in the financial reporting process. Executive management is now explicitly responsible for establishing and maintaining a system of internal control over financial reporting and conducting an annual assessment of the same. The CEO and CFO must certify the accuracy of financial reports filed with the SEC under the risk of criminal penalties and fines. Other members of the executive management team are responsible for the new requirements relating to codes of ethics, record retention, insider trading, whistleblower policies, as well as other legal and human resource issues. While the Act does not specifically mention any requirements of managers and supporting staff, these individuals generally have been directly responsible for most of the additional work that is required for initial and subsequent ongoing compliance, and they must adhere to the same ethical standards of executive management.

Companies have experienced significant increases in costs and time necessary to achieve and maintain compliance with the provisions of the Act and the related regulatory changes. Unequivocally, the most significant cost increases have been related to the external auditor attestation of internal control over financial reporting and the internal and external cost of complying with the provisions of Section 404 of the Act. The cost of compliance has varied mainly based on the size of the company, the number of operations, and the complexity of the business, but nonetheless remains significant for most organizations.

Initial implementation of the Act's provisions for internal controls over financial reporting (Section 404) and executive financial statement certification (Section 302) has undoubtedly been time consuming and costly. The daunting requirements and evolving landscape in year one forced most organizations to initially take a short-term minimum requirement approach to compliance and forego process improvement and technology implementation opportunities. Today, those same companies are seeking to reduce the cost of ongoing compliance while realizing greater benefits. In moving beyond initial compliance, organizations should view the mandated changes as an opportunity to revitalize business practices, drive improved performance, and boost investor confidence in an effort to generate a return on their investments in initial and ongoing compliance.

Prior to passage of the Act, CFOs and chief auditors often sought to focus on value-added activities such as top-line initiatives, strategic acquisitions, and operational improvements. In today's compliance environment where internal controls, which were previously regarded as secondary considerations, are front and center, the challenge is to identify ways to help Finance remain a valued partner to the business in an environment of increased governance. The following activities can help Finance continue to deliver value to stakeholders while ensuring continued compliance:

Finance Checklist: Compliance Activities that Deliver Value

☐ **Identify the enterprise strategy and communicate it throughout the Finance organization.**

Control remediation and process improvement should meet short-term goals and deliver long-term value. An organization's financial objectives are typically a combination of liquidity and working capital optimization, profitability, and growth. The strategic goals of senior management should be understood by Finance and incorporated into everyday activities. Consider the risk implications of the enterprise strategy and counsel management accordingly.

☐ **Develop a finance strategy to support the enterprise strategy.**
Reevaluate existing key metrics to address crucial Sarbanes-Oxley processes. Identify internal and external stakeholders and the information they need to make insightful decisions. Define, develop, and deploy measurements to satisfy information objectives such as key performance indicators and balanced scorecards. Benchmark against industry leaders and key competitors to establish a performance baseline. Then set goals and define a plan to achieve them.

☐ **Generate a capacity to provide analytical and consultative services.**
Remove non-value-added processes that were identified during Section 404 documentation. Develop an analytical and consulting capacity within the finance function. This competency is critical to transformation. Measure your own processes. Simplify and streamline transaction and reporting procedures through shared services, outsourcing, and accelerated close methodologies.

☐ **Leverage technology to deliver and distribute results.**
Avoid manual workarounds and reduce the cost of ongoing compliance through use of technology. Use automation as a key enabler to transformation. Leverage the capabilities of existing ERP system(s) and integrate wherever practical. Eliminate spreadsheets as a focal point of the reporting process by implementing consolidation and reporting packages. Consider Business Intelligence and Web-based distribution (XBRL) applications to improve the timeliness and accessibility of critical information.

MOVING BEYOND INITIAL COMPLIANCE

Sarbanes-Oxley accelerated filers spent countless hours and resources on initial compliance and in preparation for the filing of their first Section 404 certification. As the focus shifts to ongoing monitoring and maintenance, organizations must avoid complacency and recognize that compliance is not a one time event. There is a significant risk of noncompliance beyond year one if an organization does not have a long-term strategy and comprehensive compliance plan implemented that will support the required quarterly and annual certifications.

Compliance planning for subsequent years necessitates a reassessment of requirements and an approach definition that differs from the first-year compliance readiness plan. A more sustainable and practical program that is based on new and/or clarified guidelines must be developed and implemented. The plan may involve the implementation of new technology and a modified focus on process and policy that will support a more efficient and cost-effective approach to ongoing compliance.

An efficient and effective infrastructure that enables repeatable, reliable activities such as documentation reviews and updates, testing, and remediation is key to ongoing compliance. Because the Act requires the linking of Section 404 monitoring efforts to quarterly reporting under Section 302, companies must have the capability to conduct quarterly evaluations and to report any changes in internal controls over financial reporting that either have or could have a material effect on the financial statements. Companies must develop the ability to keep their assessment of internal controls over financial reporting current throughout the year. An organization cannot wait until the end of the fiscal year to evaluate changes in internal control for their annual assessments.

To maintain a strong control environment and derive the maximum value from an ongoing compliance program, the answers to the following questions should be continuously evaluated:

- Are you satisfied that there are no critical gaps and overlaps in the ownership of your financial reporting processes and in the underlying internal controls?

- Are you utilizing Section 404 documentation to identify opportunities to build in quality, reduce costs, and gain efficiencies, while reducing financial risk?

- Do you have an appropriate structure and detailed plan for ensuring continued compliance with Sections 302 and 404?

Good governance, as evidenced by an effective system of internal control, and adding value to the business do not have to be conflicting objectives. Many forward-thinking organizations have recognized the compatibility of the two goals and have incorporated both perspectives into their planning and compliance programs (see Figure 1.1).

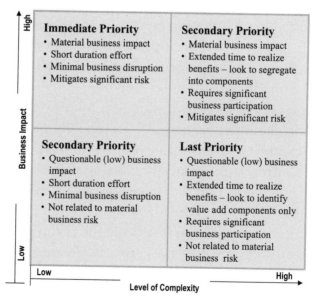

EXHIBIT 1.1   PRIORITIZATION BASED ON BUSINESS IMPACT AND LEVEL OF COMPLEXITY

Best practice considerations for ongoing compliance plans include:

- ☐ Modify compliance approach (based on the SEC Releases 5/05, 5/06, 12/06) to adopt a more risk-based topdown approach
- ☐ Develop a formal, detailed ongoing compliance plan
- ☐ Define the compliance organization structure and roles/ responsibilities
- ☐ Communicate the ongoing compliance plan to the external auditor
- ☐ Communicate the ongoing compliance plan to employees
- ☐ Develop a practical, comprehensive integrated testing plan
- ☐ Reduce testing through key control review/rationalization, based on risk assessment, control automation, and eliminate redundant controls
- ☐ Implement a compliance management tool
- ☐ Implement a control monitoring tool
- ☐ Develop an ERM strategy and plan
- ☐ Identify and implement business process improvement opportunities

Reevaluating the Compliance Program

One of the intended results of the Act was a heightened process owner awareness of financial controls and risks, as well as increased responsibility and accountability for those controls and risks. In year one, compliance documentation and testing was often managed and/or performed by external resources, which prevented process owners from fully embracing ownership of the control environment. To encourage greater internal resource involvement, the ongoing compliance plan should be designed to drive greater awareness through continued education/training as well as documentation and testing approval. Specifically, each organization should reevaluate its compliance program from four perspectives: ongoing compliance, remediation prioritization, process improvement, and operational structure and efficiency.

Ongoing Compliance Considerations

The following checklist summarizes the key principles that should be considered when planning and developing an ongoing compliance strategy:

Ongoing Compliance Strategy Checklist

☐ **Communicate a positive "tone at the top."**

The "tone at the top" significantly influences behavior throughout the organization, so certifying officers and senior executives should continually reinforce executive support and commitment to reliable financial reporting and continuous improvement and strengthening of the internal control structure and environment. The executive management tone will drive the success of ongoing compliance efforts. If management projects compliance is a burden, it will be perceived as a burden by employees, and much of the value will be lost. Compliance objectives may still be met; however, control breakdowns may occur more frequently, and the opportunity to recognize value from process improvements will most likely be forfeited.

☐ **Develop a supportive organizational structure.**

Adequate organizational support is critical to successful compliance in year two and beyond. An organizational structure that supports ongoing compliance should be defined and established, and the role of internal audit (where applicable) should be specifically outlined. Organizations should consider integrating the annual audit test plan with Sections 302 and 404 certification testing.

☐ **Reinforce the roles and responsibilities of process owners.**

The importance of the process owners' roles in the success of ongoing compliance cannot be overstated. Businesses can hire teams of external auditors and consultants to design, implement, and test systems of internal control, but they cannot ensure that those systems will be properly used and internal controls will be followed once they exit. Because process owners are accountable for the existence and effectiveness of internal controls, their roles and responsibilities in the ongoing compliance process should be clearly defined. Only then can accountability and control ownership be truly reinforced. An effective self-assessment process can assist in facilitating this reinforcement and help ensure that any control breakdowns are detected early and corrected.

☐ **Invest in compliance education and training.**

Continuous compliance education and training is vital to the success of an ongoing compliance program. Employees need to receive sufficient training on overall company compliance requirements and be educated about their individual roles in the compliance process in order to perform their jobs well and support the organization in meeting the requirements of the Act on an ongoing basis.

☐ **Implement a continuous monitoring and maintenance process.**

Because Sections 302, 404, and 409 each require ongoing compliance, every organization should design and implement a detailed continuous monitoring and maintenance process. This will help ensure that any identified remediation is completed in a timely manner. Organizations can take advantage of numerous software applications that have built-in monitoring capabilities and/or implement internal control self-assessments. Any tools that are used to facilitate the process will be dependent upon the knowledge base and commitment of employees in the organization.

☐ **Eliminate redundant closing and financial reporting activities.**

Organizations should review their current closing and financial reporting procedures and compare them against Section 302 and Section 404 certification requirements. A consolidated checklist/schedule can then be developed to enable the most efficient process and eliminate redundant activities.

☐ **Implement a process change procedure.**

Section 302 requires disclosure of any changes that materially affect internal control over financial reporting. A formal process change recognition and update procedure will help ensure timely quarterly disclosure, an efficient annual certification process, and continued confidence in the internal control environment supporting financial reporting.

☐ **Implement process improvement.**

During the initial compliance effort, a vast amount of process and control information was obtained and documented. Organizations can utilize this knowledge to foster positive change and potentially realize a return on the compliance investsment. Value can be recognized through process improvement, control remediation, and expansion beyond compliance through the development or enhancement of enterprise risk management and corporate governance programs.

REMEDIATION PRIORITIZATION

Prioritizing compliance and remediation efforts is crucial to the certification of financial reports, the annual management assessment of internal control over financial reporting, and the related external auditor attestation engagement. Remediation efforts should be designed to improve the efficiency and productivity of operating processes as well as to strengthen internal controls. Each internal control remediation plan should address not only how the corrective action improves the overall control environment, but also how it streamlines transaction process flow.

The timing of remediation efforts should also be considered. Companies should determine to what extent remediation could be conducted in conjunction with compliance activity. It is a best practice to plan for parallel documentation, control gap identification, gap remediation, and testing for both initial and ongoing compliance, because parallel execution can have a dramatic impact on the cost and the timeline of compliance efforts.

The first step in effectively coordinating various remediation requirements is to categorize them by type of improvement. Category examples include the following:

Checklist: Control improvements

☐ Mitigate missing or deficient controls

☐ Eliminate unnecessary or redundant controls

☐ Minimize process risks

☐ Eliminate policy and/or authorization deficiencies

☐ Establish control process metrics

☐ Eliminate manual controls (automate)

Checklist: Sarbanes-Oxley compliance and financial reporting improvements

☐ Establish Sarbanes-Oxley reporting package

☐ Establish standardization across financial processes and financial reporting (internal and external)

Checklist: Productivity improvements

☐ Eliminate non-value-added tasks/activities

☐ Automate manual activities/processes

☐ Establish universal data and/or process standards

☐ Update/revise policies

☐ Align business activities and efforts with perceived value

Improvement opportunities should then be prioritized based on business impact and complexity (see Figure 1.1). *High-impact improvements* address material business issues that can be accomplished in a short duration with minimal business disruption. They mitigate significant business risk and typically yield results quickly. Implementation should not extend beyond 90 days. *Medium-impact improvements* also focus on material business issues; however, they require an extended period of time and strong participation from the business. Implementation will typically take between three to six months.

Prioritizing remediation activities based on process improvement opportunities will not only reduce the organization's latency in reporting and disclosures, but also advance Finance's position as a valued business partner.

Process Improvement

Documentation efforts required for Section 404 compliance have prompted many companies to take the first step in business process improvements (e.g., documentation of current processes, and identification of redundancies and inefficiencies). As control remediation continues, companies are well positioned to incorporate additional process improvements into their compliance infrastructures.

Operational Structure and Efficiency

An increased pressure to do things faster, better, and more cost effectively has prompted companies to pursue various strategies to improve operational effectiveness. What functions should be performed within the business units? Who should select, purchase, and operate the supporting technologies? When should business units be free to choose operating standards, and when should Corporate mandate consistency? These questions are answered differently based on a company's operating style, industry, and market focus.

Because there are benefits to centralization and decentralization, companies should closely examine both approaches before making any operational changes (see Figure 1.2).

Benefits of Centralization/Standardization

- Less redundancy in operations

- Leverage of management time and attention

- Economies of scale

- Easier implementation of best-practice approaches

- More defined career paths for professionals in support functions

- Reduced maintenance costs and effort

- More efficient utilization of IT resources (e.g., technical infrastructure, application support and licensing, and modifications)

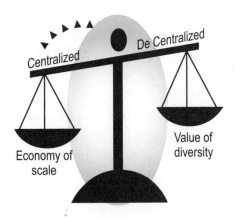

Exhibit 1.2   Centralization vs. De-centralization

Benefits of Decentralization/Customization

- Processes and systems can be tailored to each business unit's unique needs.

- Local systems can be more responsive to changes in business conditions.

- Local operations can help foster a culture of ownership.

- Local operations that are integrated through a monthly feed of summarized financial information to Corporate can be more easily incorporated or divested.

While there are benefits to decentralization, compliance requirements driven by the Act will likely increase the focus on economies of scale and therefore require greater centralization. The expense and time required to annually review process documentation and retest will increase with each separate department engaged in auditable activity. This will be particularly true where operations are not only separate, but also vary in terms of systems, formats, and process design.

Centralization is not an easy change. Companies are often reluctant to move away from their decentralized structures (even if they know they are ineffective) because the social, technical, and financial costs of change can be high. Nonetheless, more organizations are finding that the additional cost of complying with the Act warrants the decision to centralize or even employ a shared services model.

Public companies spent significantly more than they had previously estimated to comply with Section 404. Informal estimates indicate annual ongoing costs for monitoring and compliance currently amount to as much as 50 to 70 percent of the initial compliance costs. Organizations should conduct operational and budget reviews to prevent future costs from skyrocketing. Companies that have maintained critical financial functions at the divisional level should reconsider centralizing those functions in order to take advantage of greater economies of scale.

Leading companies have shifted Sarbanes-Oxley efforts from "project" to "process," moving toward a more sustainable infrastructure that will support ongoing financial management operations. Immediately addressing the four critical areas of *ongoing compliance, remediation prioritization, process improvements,* and *operational structures and efficiency* will help organizations leverage the knowledge obtained through compliance activities and capitalize on the opportunity to improve business processes, while maintaining a solid control environment. This approach will enable Finance to add value while ensuring good corporate governance.

2

OPTIMIZING COMPLIANCE EFFORTS

CURRENT COMPLIANCE CHALLENGES

For most companies, achieving Section 404 compliance has proven to be more challenging, and more costly, than they initially anticipated. In most cases, initial and year-two compliance efforts strained company resources while still leaving internal control issues, causing many organizations to take a bare-minimum approach to meeting the requirements of the Act. As a result, companies are currently facing the following challenges:

- Most compliance activity time continues to be spent on remediation, leaving little time to develop a long-term compliance plan or to create more efficient processes.

- The cost of compliance has actually grown in some cases as a result of a substantial increase in material weakness disclosures and restatements.

- Many organizations do not have an appropriate infrastructure and implementation plan sufficient to sustain compliance, minimize risks, and reduce costs.

Therefore, any discussion about sustaining compliance should be focused on developing a plan that facilitates cost reduction/minimization, increased reliability/confidence with financial results, and delivering benefits/value.

FUTURE STATE OPPORTUNITY: COMPLIANCE OPTIMIZATION

Companies need to optimize their ongoing compliance programs in the future to improve control effectiveness, realize cost savings, and provide tangible benefits to the organization. This entails defining the organizational structure, roles and responsibilities, ongoing compliance process, training and communication (including the audit committee and board of directors), reporting, and incorporating the use of technology within the ongoing compliance process. Specifically, a comprehensive, long-term program should be structured as shown in Exhibit 2.1.

EXHIBIT 2.1   COMPREHENSIVE COMPLIANCE PROGRAM PYRAMID

Governance

A good governance approach requires that the tone at the top be established and continuously reinforced. The organization should develop an integrated compliance strategy, and objectives should be clearly outlined and communicated. Senior executives should seek to establish and foster a culture of integrity and high ethical standards. Ultimately, developed governance policies as well as adherence to these established guidelines should be continuously monitored, and ownership, responsibility, and accountability for good governance and internal controls should be embedded throughout the culture of the organization.

Enterprise Risk Management

The creation of a comprehensive ERM program requires the following activities and considerations:

- Identify and assess risk

- Develop a risk-response strategy

- Document control activities

- Apply risk management to gain competitive advantage

(See Chapter 3 for additional discussion.)

Compliance

This component requires that the organization focus on ensuring adherence to all applicable laws and regulations. The objective/focus should be on efficiency coupled with accuracy. A fully integrated, streamlined, efficient process leads to cost reduction/minimization and potential increase in shareholder value (see Exhibit 2.2).

Compliance Optimization Process – Major Components

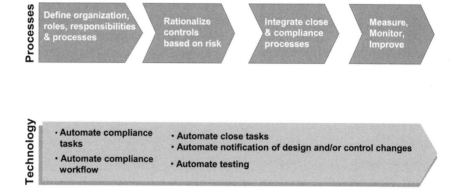

EXHIBIT 2.2   COMPLIANCE OPTIMIZATION PROCESS—MAJOR COMPONENTS

ISSUES TO CONSIDER
WHEN OPTIMIZING COMPLIANCE

Four years after passage of the Sarbanes-Oxley Act, U.S. corporations are still grappling with the complex array of regulations and the enormous costs required to comply with them. While many gray areas remain, forward-thinking companies can reduce the burden of ongoing compliance by taking action to improve the efficiency and accuracy of their financial processes.

The following commonly reported deficiencies and compliance issues should be carefully considered when developing a monitoring and maintenance plan that will sustain compliance:

Checklist: Issues to Consider when Developing Monitoring/Maintenance Plan

☐ **Financial Close**

This process is typically complex and involves high-risk activities, which are performed in a short time period. In many cases, organizations lack formal defined and documented processes and controls for financial close activity. Ongoing compliance is at risk in this situation. A major compliance focus is on the process of providing information reported on the financial statements. Organizations should seek to include automation wherever possible in this process, integrate the financial close and compliance processes, as well as continuously seek to strengthen financial reporting and disclosure procedures.

☐ **Reporting and Disclosure**

Many organizations continue to demonstrate a lack of process definition, resource dedication, technical knowledge/expertise/skill set, and an adequately documented process, as well as evidence of approval regarding financial reporting and disclosure activity. Similar to the financial close process, there is a major focus on the methods that organizations utilize to report and disclose critical information regarding the organizations financial position.

☐ **Information Technology Controls**

Many organizations found they had inadequate documentation of IT controls. In particular, companies lacked sufficient detail in such general control areas as backup, recovery, and program change control. Inadequate documentation must now be supplemented with enough detail to reflect a stable control environment. Inefficiency of manual controls and the inability to automate these controls quickly enough to meet initial compliance requirements are also frequently cited.

☐ **Post-Merger Integration**

It is generally very difficult to maintain a strong system of internal control during merger and acquisition activity because of the merging of people, processes, and technology and the time constraints placed on the resources involved in the transaction. As a result, organizations often neglect the control environment, creating a high risk of control weaknesses, gaps, and/or deficiencies.

☐ **Outsourced Functions**

Many organizations have outsourced one or more basic functions or business processes. In most cases, the process activity has had a significant impact on financial reporting. The organization should request a SAS 70 Type II letter that clearly outlines the expectations of the vendor and the requirements of the contents of the documents provided. The certifying organization must be able to obtain adequate information about the vendor's control environment and the controls over financial reporting in order for management and the external auditors to certify and attest to their overall control environment (including the outsourced activity).

☐ **Personnel**

Many companies experience deficiencies in the segregation of duties, staffing, and training. For example, many companies simply do not have the necessary Finance/Accounting staff to meet their needs, so individuals with insufficient skills and inadequate experience are often performing critical tasks. In addition, the same person may perform multiple tasks, such as approving and paying invoices, duties that should be segregated between individuals.

Many companies disclosed (and are still attempting to overcome) these issues and deficiencies. These organizations should periodically review their remediation plans and timing with their external auditors and provide regular status reports on their progress. Depending on the severity of the identified deficiencies, the external auditor typically expects the company to complete remediation by the following year-end. Companies can effectively address such deficiencies through on-going compliance planning activities summarized as follows:

Checklist: Steps to Address On-going Compliance Planning

☐ **Take a practical approach when testing for fraud.**

Companies should evaluate their organization based on such factors as size and industry and concentrate their efforts on areas with the greatest potential/risk for fraud.

☐ **Focus on and evaluate company-wide controls first.**

Controls are used to prevent and detect potential errors in financial reporting. In the past, many organizations focused on a wide range of controls simultaneously in order to rapidly comply with Act requirements. Auditors and organizations should refocus their efforts by looking at the entity-level control landscape and drilling down only where absolutely necessary.

☐ **Automate controls wherever possible to minimize year-to-year testing.**

Replacing manual controls with automated controls strengthens the control environment and reduces the amount of testing required on an annual basis.

☐ **Leverage past compliance efforts.**

When planning their ongoing compliance efforts, companies should review past compliance initiatives to better maximize their results.

☐ **Integrate audits of internal controls with audits of financial statements.**

This helps minimize redundancy when companies conduct testing and gather evidence, resulting in significant savings in time and cost.

Ongoing Compliance Plan

The initial Sarbanes-Oxley compliance plan should be modified to eliminate the onetime efforts of initial compliance such as pilot programs and full documentation requirements, and should be refined to include a current review and risk assessment. In addition, ongoing compliance planning should also include analyses of software automation opportunities, general controls documentation requirements, outsourced functions, and process changes that have occurred since the prior compliance period. This process should be conducted through interviews with key members of the applicable management team and key process owners. Using a thorough control self-assessment questionnaire can be an effective tool to address all relevant issues in the risk assessment process.

After completing the risk assessment of the control environment, the ongoing compliance plan should be modified to include the risk assessment results. With this data as a foundation, a specific work plan with well-defined roles and responsibilities, including compliance owners, should be developed. This plan should also include:

- Specific tasks to be completed and their sequence

- Expected duration of the tasks

- Task assignments

- Expected outcomes from the tasks listed

- Critical milestones

Next, the following steps should be performed:

- Define roles and responsibilities

- Appoint an overall compliance owner or project manager

- Define the role of the internal audit function in ongoing compliance

- Define the roles of process owners and business units

- Finalize a training and communication plan

- Define the status-reporting hierarchy, structure, content, and frequency

- Determine the role of technology and software

In addition, the methods and procedures for the following should be defined:

- Process review

- Documentation review and update

- Policy review and update

- Control issue escalation

- Gap analysis

- Remediation and prioritization

Ongoing Reporting

For SOX compliance, all future quarterly (Section 302) and annual (Section 404) financial reports must include a certification executed by the CEO and the CFO. Section 404 mandates that required annual reports include: (1) an internal control report stating management's responsibility for internal control and management's assessment of internal controls for the most recent fiscal year; and (2) the external auditor's attestation to, and report on, management's assessments.

To expedite the final reporting process, information generated by the project team and process owners should be utilized to draft the required certification report. The report cannot be finalized until the remediation plan and any additional testing is completed. Preparation of the documents in anticipation of the results of any required retesting will facilitate the final report process. The draft report should be provided to the steering committee and the audit committee for review and comment.

Once remediation (if applicable) and required control activity testing is complete, the draft certification disclosures and management's assessment of internal control over financial reporting can be finalized for inclusion in the required quarterly or annual report. The final certifications and assessment reports—along with a final report of findings from the project team indicating the status of internal control over financial reporting and the resolution of both the remediation plan and corrective action log—should be presented to the steering committee, audit committee, and certifying executives for final review, modification, and approval.

Customize Your Compliance Plan

There is no "one-size-fits-all" solution for ongoing compliance. Many different factors affect the organizational structure, role and responsibility definition, and the monitoring and reporting processes that comprise an organization's compliance program. When such a plan is developed, the long-term compliance strategy should be clearly outlined and evaluated to ensure that it is forward-looking and aligned with overall company objectives and other tactical initiatives that may be underway. Specific factors that can influence your compliance strategy/plan are summarized in the following checklist:

Checklist: Factors that Influence a Compliance Strategy/Plan

☐ **Culture.** Is the organization ready for change?

- ☐ **Organizational complexity.** Is the organization centralized or decentralized? Geographically dispersed?
- ☐ **Organizational structure.** What is the company reporting hierarchy?
- ☐ **Current status and focus of compliance efforts.** Is the current compliance plan integrated with other company initiatives and requirements as well as the overall company strategy and objectives?
- ☐ **Percentage of manual processes.** How much control automation exists?
- ☐ **Sophistication of current technology.** Are disparate systems present?
- ☐ **Resource availability and skill sets.** Do you have the internal bandwidth and expertise to execute an effective compliance program?

After examining the company's compliance strategy, consider integrating the ongoing compliance program with other strategic initiatives such as business performance management (BPM), enterprise risk management (ERM), and business process improvement/automation. An integrated framework not only minimizes costs but also improves information quality and increases transparency, which, in turn, enables more proactive decision making and strengthens the overall control environment. A comprehensive approach can also maximize shareholder value. ERM, when combined with BPM, provides a complete view of past, present, and future performance, which encourages the proactive management of the business and supports rapid decision making.

RIGHT-SIZING BEST PRACTICES

In year three of compliance and beyond, companies should shift their focus from implementation to sustainability and adopt tools and practices that will facilitate the right-sizing of their existing compliance program through increased efficiency and streamlined business processes. Consider the following when defining the scope of your compliance efforts and building a sustainable, cost-effective process.

Outsourcing

Now that all processes have been formally and thoroughly documented, many organizations are in a better position to look closer at process improvements options such as outsourcing. Once viewed as primarily a tactical, cost-cutting measure, outsourcing has matured into a sophisticated and proven business process improvement measure that can also improve the control environment and streamline compliance activities. Outsourcing a specific process or function such as Accounts Payable or Accounts Receivable can strengthen a deficient or weak control environment by enhancing segregation of duties and increasing control automation. Outsourcing select processes to the appropriate partner can provide an organization with a method of reducing ongoing compliance costs through greater efficiency as well as reducing risk. In addition, outsourcing can provide a greater process visibility, enhance control, and ensure the accuracy of financial statements.

Currently, the leading outsource providers are very sophisticated and offer high quality, efficiency, and increased work capacity through streamlined processes and advanced technology.

Control Testing

The objective of control testing is to provide an appropriate basis for management to determine the operational effectiveness of the key internal controls identified during risk assessment and documentation. The results from the test procedures will form the basis of, and support, management's assertion on internal control over financial reporting included in annual reports. The external auditor may also review the results of testing during their attestation of, and report on, management's assessment of internal control over financial reporting.

Appropriate testing procedures include inquiry, observation, inspection, performance of control activities, and examination of evidence necessary to support account balances. Because controls should be tested at both the entity level and the transaction or application level, it is a best practice to integrate test plans and reduce the number of controls through the following:

- Risk assessment

- Rationalization

- Process standardization/centralization

- Process improvement

- Automation

Control Automation

Control automation can reduce testing, eliminate manual controls, increase preventive controls while decreasing detective controls, and strengthen the control environment. It can also significantly reduce costs and improve the timeliness and quality of status reporting. Findings in a recent ongoing compliance survey conducted by Parson Consulting, IBM Business Consulting Services, and APQC, an international research organization, revealed a significant cost differential between top- and bottom-performing respondents based on how each group handled the management and reporting of the compliance process.

Noteworthy cost contributors included systems costs and the number of full-time equivalents (FTEs) required to execute the compliance process. Top-performing organizations typically implemented technology to support the compliance process and/or had automated controls as part of their ongoing compliance efforts. As a result, cost savings were generated through a reduction in one or more of the following:

- Number of FTEs involved in the compliance process

- Control violation identification time

- Internal and external reporting time

The strategic use of technology can help companies contain the cost and effort required to achieve regulatory compliance; however, an integrated approach should be adopted to fully achieve such benefits. Several software vendors currently offer integrated solutions that can help organizations complete compliance requirements more efficiently (see Chapter 4).

Accelerate the Close Process

Accelerated reporting requirements have prompted many organizations to examine their close process and identify methods to increase the accuracy and timeliness of financial information. Software can automate compliance and the close process by unifying financial reporting, close tasks, and internal controls, thereby reducing the risk of material weakness disclosures and financial restatements. By capturing and securing all transactions and documents associated with close and compliance activities, these tools can preserve data integrity and reduce costs through process improvement. While technology can certainly be an enabler, it cannot successfully reduce the close process by itself. A faster close can only be accomplished by improving the processes that collect and feed data into the system.

Integrated ERM and BPM Solution

Compliance can be successfully used as a platform for the development and implementation of an ERM strategy and plan. An organization should adopt a risk-based, top-down approach to compliance by applying a formal ERM framework. Most organizations applied limited risk management concepts during initial compliance and only utilized this model as far as what is dictated by Sarbanes-Oxley requirements. As a result, these companies have not appropriately identified and considered all of the risks and/or events that may positively or negatively impact their businesses.

Organizations should begin to more seriously consider risk as part of their daily operations. Integrating risk with performance measurement initiatives such as BPM can provide a realistic expectation of future performance by monitoring risk indicators that will alert management to changes in the risk profile. Tracking a limited number of key performance indicators and key risk indicators gives management the concise, actionable information needed to determine how the company is currently performing and may perform in the future. However, such proactive management of performance—and the creation of shareholder value—is optimal only when BPM and ERM are fully integrated.

Integrating ongoing compliance activities with risk management, performance management, automation, and process improvement activities—and aligning all initiatives with overall company strategy and objectives—will result in increased efficiency, a stronger control environment, and a lower cost of operations and compliance.

THE ROLE OF INTERNAL AUDIT: BALANCING THE COMPLIANCE AND AUDIT FUNCTIONS

Increased compliance requirements have demanded a great deal of attention from internal audit departments. Internal auditors, with their expertise in business process analysis, control testing, and risk management, have been involved in various compliance initiatives that have led to a dramatic increase in workload without an increase in resources. Many organizations allocated as much as 50 percent or more of their internal audit groups to initial Section

404 work. The end result was predictable: traditional internal audit work—such as assessing controls, generating value, and improving operations—was often neglected in order to meet the more pressing demands of regulatory compliance. In many cases, the internal audit group possessed more controls expertise than any other part of the company, and therefore, appropriately took on the majority of the compliance burden. Yet such an unbalanced deployment of internal audit resources is not sustainable or practical for most organizations.

As companies move beyond year three of Act compliance, they should seek to rebalance internal audit activities and restructure the function's role to maximize its overall effectiveness and minimize ongoing compliance cost. In addition, specific consideration and attention should be given to ensuring that a conflict does not exist between any third parties performing internal audit outsourcing and control gap remediation support.

Meeting compliance requirements as well as maintaining compliance is obviously important, but not to the neglect of internal audit's standard auditing responsibilities. Failure to address key strategic and operational risks in conjunction with compliance risk undermines the value of internal audit and exposes the company to greater operational and financial risks. Today, more than ever, a properly structured internal audit function can be a tremendous benefit to an organization, impacting not only regulatory compliance but also operational excellence. Companies can work toward obtaining a balanced, high-performing internal audit function by taking the steps outlined as follows.

Checklist: Internal Audit

☐ **Define internal audit's role to again include operational risk as well as compliance support.**

   Focusing internal audit on the basic audit function can better position the group to participate in risk management activity, strategize on how to streamline operations, and enhance competitiveness through cost reductions and greater shareholder value. Audit work should be thoughtfully balanced between financial, operational, strategic, compliance, and information technology risk assessment. This may be accomplished by potentially transitioning some of the first-year compliance responsibility to business units and process owners, which would allow internal audit to devote more time to its traditional responsibilities.

- [ ] **Determine whether the internal audit department is properly staffed and contains the proper skill mix to successfully perform its responsibilities.**

Compliance and the need for knowledgeable resources to assist with compliance plan implementation and continuous monitoring has created a shortage of available qualified resources. Many individual company Section 404 certifications contained disclosures on issues or weaknesses with the capabilities and/or competency of the accounting and finance group. In addition, many companies have developed an ongoing compliance plan that involves utilizing the internal audit group in some capacity. Each company should confirm that the appropriate number of qualified resources (based on the ongoing compliance plan) exist within both the accounting and internal audit groups. This will help ensure that organizations are able to execute the company's compliance plan and verify compliance with the Act from a personnel capability standpoint.

- [ ] **Leverage testing conducted independently by internal audit in order to minimize external audit testing and costs.**

External auditors cannot completely rely on the *results* of management testing when formulating their opinion regarding the control environment; however, the SEC/PCAOB pronouncements continue to affirm that external auditors can and should rely on the work of independent third parties. Therefore, auditors can rely on testing conducted by internal auditors if the testing is independent of management testing. If this structure is adopted, external auditors can reduce the amount of their control testing, which would reduce external audit fees and encourage organizations to capitalize on the concentrated skill sets within their internal audit groups.

The new compliance requirements have challenged companies to redefine the structure, staffing, and role of their internal audit groups. Organizations should determine the most efficient, cost-effective way to structure and use the internal audit function, while giving specific consideration to how the group can be best utilized to facilitate ongoing compliance cost reduction.

THE EVOLVING ROLE OF THE AUDIT COMMITTEE

The role of the audit committee has expanded and changed at an unprecedented rate as a result of the passing of the Sarbanes-Oxley Act and an increased focus on corporate governance. Today's audit committee members are empowered and more influential, but they also have increased responsibilities and greater accountability. Rules outlining the composition of the audit committee and its independence have emerged; however, rules alone will not provide the foundation needed to build the relationships and leadership that will ensure the committee's effectiveness and the integrity of a company's financial information.

In today's environment, boards of directors and audit committee members are asking significantly more questions of management in order to more thoroughly understand a company's business, risks, and control environment. An increased need for information, driven by the need to make informed decisions, requires audit committees to spend more time preparing and interacting with management, external auditors, and internal auditors in order to fully understand a company's strategy and approach to compliance.

Many audit committees have not adopted best practices, despite the regulatory microscope under which committee members currently operate. The percentage of committees implementing best practices is surprisingly low for a group that plays such an important role in the welfare and integrity of a company. Audit committees can implement several best practices to enhance their performance and role within organizations.

Checklist: Audit Committee Best Practices

☐ **Don't do management's job.**

Committee members should ask appropriate questions to understand management's long- and short-term approach to initial and ongoing compliance to ensure that an effective compliance program is in place. Ultimately, the audit committee's role should be to understand how management has designed and intends to implement the company's compliance plan. Because this group has the last plan review opportunity, the committee has a responsibility to make sure management is doing what it needs to in order to safeguard shareholder value. Such knowledge should create a comfort level with the strategy and plan that will allow the audit committee to support management in the communication and implementation of compliance initiatives. If a comfort level with the plan does not exist, the audit committee should guide the organization in revising the strategy and/or plan in order to fully support it.

☐ **Support the tone at the top.**

The overall effectiveness of the control environment depends on setting and maintaining the tone at the top, which is shaped by executive management. Given its expanded role, the audit committee represents the ultimate tone at the top, and therefore needs to demonstrate support for the compliance program both internally to all employees (from senior management to process owners) as well as externally to shareholders and investors. This support can only be demonstrated if audit committee members have a good understanding and comfort level with the compliance strategy and plan.

☐ **Allow adequate meeting time.**

The expanded role of the Audit Committee has warranted, in many cases, more frequent and lengthy meetings in order to adequately provide the financial and regulatory oversight outlined by the Act. Ample time should be allotted for discussing the status of the company's compliance program and examining both control strengths and weaknesses.

☐ **Monitor control gap remediation efforts against plans.**

Audit committees should review the gap remediation strategy and plan and have, at a minimum, a general understanding of existing control gaps as well as the effect this may have on the company's compliance status and certification. Members should be prepared to provide or arrange guidance if remediation prioritization assistance is required. In addition, gap remediation activity should be closely monitored for progress and completion.

☐ **Support cost-effective initiatives that strengthen internal controls.**

The high costs of ongoing compliance have sharpened the focus and need for initiatives that can streamline the compliance process and improve the overall internal control environment. Audit committee members should review and inquire regarding compliance efforts to ensure the company has created an ongoing compliance plan that not only concentrates on strengthening the control environment but also focuses on receiving optimum value and/or return on compliance investment.

Here are five important questions audit committees should be asking to help organizations effectively identify and address compliance risks, challenges, and opportunities:

Checklist: Five Critical Questions Audit Committees Should Ask:

☐ **Is the company's relationship with its auditor free of conflict?**

The Sarbanes-Oxley Act strictly prohibits registered public accountants who are conducting a financial statement audit from performing nonauditing services such as the design and implementation of financial information systems, appraisals, valuations, fairness opinions, internal audit outsourcing, and management functions. Even if a company is not subject to the Act, the audit committee should examine relationships with outside auditors to ensure they are independent and objective, so the company avoids actual conflicts and perceived conflicts of interest.

☐ **What is the long-term strategy for ongoing compliance, and does it focus on cost reduction?**

Organizations can minimize costs by designing and implementing a comprehensive ongoing compliance program, employing process enhancements, and selectively using technology. Such investments can actually generate a return through increased overall operational efficiency resulting from streamlined processes. Furthermore, it is estimated that organizations that adopt comprehensive compliance management architecture may spend as much as 50 percent less on ongoing compliance than those that do not have such a plan.

☐ **How is the organization integrating Sarbanes-Oxley compliance with other compliance requirements?**

Maintaining separate systems or procedures for different compliance requirements can create silos that are difficult to manage across the organization. An integrated compliance framework will streamline processes, eliminate duplicate work, provide more effective risk management, and reduce overall compliance costs.

☐ **Does the company have a formal Risk Management program? If not, is there a plan in place to build one or expand based on Sarbanes-Oxley compliance?**

With a comprehensive, integrated ERM framework, all identified risks and controls can be more effectively managed across business units, functions, and activities, including those affecting Act compliance. Implementing a common framework to address all regulatory requirements can provide considerable savings through greater operational efficiency over the cost of multiple stand-alone initiatives and responses.

☐ **Does the organization have a formally approved and tested business continuity plan?**

Recent disasters have left companies with a heightened awareness of their vulnerability to business disruptions and the associated costs. A company should have a business continuity plan in place to help the organization operate in the event of a natural or man-made disaster. Business continuity planning is focused primarily on the recovery of cross-functional business operations and resources as opposed to computer systems. Engaging in such planning will allow organizations to minimize the risk of revenue loss resulting from disruptions in business processes, customer service, and/or lack of regulatory compliance.

Audit committees are charged with the task of providing the leadership required for a company to achieve the highest corporate governance standards. This task has been complicated, in part, by the high costs of both initial and ongoing compliance. Estimates approximate that in many cases between 40 and 70 percent of the cost of initial compliance is currently being spent by organizations on ongoing compliance.

Because most CFOs will not condone such a high level of expense for the long term, companies must quickly find ways to minimize costs. The Audit Committee plays a vital role in focusing companies on the need to examine their compliance efforts and identify opportunities to gain efficiency. The Audit Committee should suggest and support initiatives and investments that will reduce ongoing compliance costs through a strengthened control environment and a streamlined compliance process.

3

THE TIME HAS COME FOR ERM

Less than a decade ago, Enterprise Risk Management (ERM) was not a major focus for most organizations. Today, it is quickly ascending to the top of the agendas of senior executives and shareholders alike as corporate scandals and globalization challenge the status quo and regulators publish new or updated requirements.

Enterprise Risk Management is a structured approach to aligning strategy, processes, people, technology, and knowledge to identify and manage uncertainties and risk. Providing a comprehensive, integrated framework that enables organizations to *proactively manage* business risk, ERM aids in the achievement of balance between business needs and risk thresholds to increase competitive advantage and shareholder value. ERM definitions tend to vary from source to source, but all contain common themes: a standard risk management process, an integrated view of risks, and a focus on relating risks to business objectives.

One would think that recent corporate scandals and fraud as well as provisions set by the Sarbanes-Oxley Act would have spurred companies to assess and improve the management and mitigation of enterprise-wide risks. Despite the plethora of internal and/or external events that could expose an organization to serious risks, companies focus much more on measuring and monitoring financial performance than on proactively measuring, analyzing, and responding to and mitigating risks—threats that could negatively impact financial performance.

A recent survey found that 61 percent of 152 senior executives from U.S. multinational companies recognize that they must improve their risk identification and assessment process in future years because of new corporate-disclosure rules. Fifty-five percent anticipate adopting risk-mitigation processes, the survey found.[1]

Most risk management experts agree that companies are generally not doing a good job of assessing and managing risk because either they lack the discipline for it or a mandate from executive management is absent. However, risk management is rapidly becoming a major area of focus, and risk areas within each organization should be analyzed. Currently, two of the prominent drivers prompting the development of a formal enterprise risk framework are:

- **Regulatory guidance.** SEC releases (May 2005 and December 2006) reference a risk-based approach to compliance. This focus serves as an excellent platform for the design and implementation of an enterprise-wide risk management program. The program does not have to be implemented throughout the entire organization concurrently, but it can be rolled out using a phased approach (e.g., business unit, geography, function).

- **Evolving roles of the Audit Committee and Board of Directors.** Since the passage of the Act, audit committee members and directors have increased responsibilities and greater accountability. This has prompted them to focus inquiries on the organization's plans for developing a formal risk management strategy and plan.

---

1. Sarbanes-Oxley Compliance Survey, PricewaterhouseCoopers, reported July 2004.

Companies that assess risk, set risk thresholds, and actively monitor and manage their risk exposure within those thresholds are better able to more accurately predict future performance. They are also more likely to achieve higher performance and/or meet financial expectations because they are better able to avoid large fluctuations in business and evade the negative consequences of unmitigated risk events.

Federal Reserve Board Governor Susan Schmidt Bies recently called on companies to adopt a "consistent, sound enterprise-wide risk management culture. By adopting such a culture, risk management is viewed as a way to keep pace with changes in risks and achieve strategic advantage rather than a mere compliance exercise, she maintains."[2] She also contends that risk management and internal control begins by "stretching the planning exercise" to consider alternative outcomes.

Ms. Bies believes "managers should be expected to evaluate the risks and controls within their authority at least annually and report the results to both the executive who oversees risk management initiatives and the board audit committee. Internal audit or another independent source should perform a separate evaluation to confirm management's assessments," she adds.

Although the percentage is declining, it is surprising how few organizations have a formal ERM program in place. Even if companies have a risk management program, often it is more informal in nature. This is shocking, given the amount of money that has been lost in the financial markets as a result of poor risk management and fraud. Gartner Inc., the research organization, estimates the figure to be $12 billion between 1992 and 2003.[3]

---

2. "Add Risk Exposure Considerations to Planning Process, Says Fed Governor," America's Community Bankers, March 1, 2005.
3. Gartner Group, as quoted in Sun Microsystems' Boardroom Minutes, 2003.

The Benefits of ERM: Value Preservation and Creation

The goal of every company is to maximize value for its shareholders. Value can certainly be created or deflated by business decisions made at the top, but it can also be created, preserved, or eroded by routine decisions that occur at every level within the organization. ERM supports value creation by helping management assess future events and respond in a manner that reduces the likelihood of outcomes that would lead to value erosion.

Successful long-term risk management enables the organization to anticipate risks resulting from opportunity, uncertainty, and hazards, which can present occasions for either value enhancement (i.e., upside risk) or value erosion (i.e., downside risk). Analysis of upside risk can provide valuable insight that management can use to plan actions that will achieve positive gains. Defensively managing downside risk through policies, procedures, and systems may help prevent behaviors that could negatively impact company performance.

A functional approach to risk management often creates silos that can be difficult to manage across the enterprise. An integrated ERM framework allows for risks to be effectively managed across business units, functions, and business activities. Employees can be empowered to own and manage risks in their respective areas.

The real value of ERM surfaces when organizations look beyond assessing risk for the sole purpose of meeting minimum regulatory requirements. A comprehensive risk management plan presents a higher value proposition. The benefits of pursuing such a solution can be numerous. A few of the main benefits include:

- **Cost savings through an integrated approach to compliance.** Overlapping requirements, which compete for company resources and management's attention, have prompted an increasing number of companies to develop a common framework for addressing all regulatory requirements. Such an integrated approach can provide considerable savings over the cost of multiple stand-alone responses by providing greater operational efficiency.

- **Optimized capital structure and allocation.** Improved estimation of a company's capital requirements is one of the most frequently cited benefits of ERM. A better understanding of risk across an organization leads to a more thorough understanding of what capital is required to support a given risk tolerance. ERM also leads to better capital allocation among business units. As risk management capabilities improve, a company can achieve a greater level of transparency, which helps boards and senior executives make more informed decisions about capital allocation as well as business mix, products, and future investments.

- **More proactive management.** ERM can help a company's board and senior management team focus their efforts on strategic decision making rather than reacting to unexpected risks. Increasing management's focus on the future based on existing information and analysis, rather than crisis management, can lead to improved decision making and a better competitive position for the company.

IMPLEMENTING ERM

A risk management framework should go beyond traditional financial accounting controls and procedures to help an organization achieve its objectives through the proactive management of business risks. Goals of the framework should include the following:

Checklist: Goals of the Risk Management Framework

- ☐ Provide the board and senior management team with a portfolio view of risk (i.e., business-unit level and entity level) to gain an understanding of how such risks are being managed.

☐ Give business areas the ability to proactively identify, assess, and report on the control level of their risks within the context of the company's overall business objectives.

☐ Support continuous process improvement and enhance shareholder value.

☐ Emphasize how individual risks interrelate, and reinforce the importance people play in the mitigation of risk.

A team of representatives from key areas of the company should be assembled to assist in establishing a formal ERM framework. This team, or a portion of it, may continue as part of a risk management organization after the initial critical framework development is completed. Management representation from throughout the organization should be included on the risk management team. Executive management buy-in and support is essential to the success of this initiative; therefore, the CEO and/or CFO should actively participate. If a compliance officer has been appointed, he or she should also be included. Depending on the organization, participation may also include representatives from the financial, accounting, legal, internal audit, information technology, human resources, actuary, and operational areas.

Once a project team has been established, the next step is to identify and assess internal and external risks to the organization in order to develop a formal ERM plan. The risk analysis should produce a risk ranking and ultimately a risk profile for the organization as well as a strategy for continuous monitoring and assessment of the documented risks.

The risk identification process can be daunting because both internal and external risks must be measured. Gauging internal risk factors like fraud and determining how to minimize such risks tends to be a bit easier than analyzing external risk factors such as economic, political, legal, market, industry, and regulatory issues and developing mitigation plans to address each. The importance of accurately predicting various risks and judging the levels of severity should not be underestimated. Credit-rating agencies and shareholders base their assessment of an organization and its future performance potential partially on the perception of the organization's ability to address and minimize risks.

The risk management plan should include the establishment of a formal risk escalation process. Many organizations evaluate risk once a year, but with a formal plan everyone is more aware of the potential hazards as well as a risk escalation process and can act accordingly. Most companies rank risk levels as high, medium, or low and may use heat-mapping (red, yellow, and green) to clearly delineate rankings. The likelihood of a risk occurring within the context of the existing control environment should also be considered.

Besides identifying the universe of possible risks and establishing a ranking for each, a risk management team usually participates in defining an organization's:

- **Risk Appetite** (i.e., the amount of risk exposure or potential adverse impact from an event the organization is willing to accept or retain). This evaluation consists of three principal elements: (1) the probable impact of a risk or event on the organization, (2) the likelihood the risk or event actually will occur, and (3) the risk-response scorecard that directs mitigating action based on the overall risk level for each risk or event.

- **Risk Response** (i.e., consideration of the appropriate response or management processes for each identified risk, as well as consideration of each risk individually and as part of the organization's overall risk portfolio). Risk response can range from avoidance to acceptance. Avoidance may be considered an acceptable option if the ability to alleviate risk is unacceptably low. Risk response usually assumes the form of mitigating risk and risk-reduction planning.

Risk mitigation helps a company better position itself to more accurately predict future performance. In doing so, the organization is now proactively addressing risk, instead of behaving reactively, when a risk materializes or threatens. If a formal risk management process is in place, the risk management team most likely has already identified and monitored the risk or threat and developed a mitigation plan that can be proactively executed.

Effectively managing risk is a vital component to an organization's success. It helps a company make more informed decisions and gain comfort that the proper steps are being taken to achieve company goals and maximize success.

ENTERPRISE RISK MANAGEMENT CYCLE

Many organizations that had not previously developed a formal ERM program are utilizing the work performed during initial Sarbanes-Oxley compliance as a platform to begin building and implementing such a plan. Ultimately, ERM should be the over-arching program, and all required compliance programs should be integrated into the overall risk management plan (see Figure 3.1).

A comprehensive ERM program should consist of the following high-level steps: Risk Identification, Risk Analysis/Quantification, Organizational Assessment, and Reporting and Monitoring.

Risk Identification

Checklist: Risk Identification Questions to Consider

- ☐ What could prevent the organization from achieving its objectives?
- ☐ Have the following types of risk been taken into account: (1) operational risks, (2) transactional risks resulting from execution error, product complexity, booking error, settlement error, delivery error/failure, or faulty documentation/contract, and (3) operational control risks resulting from exceeding limits, rogue trading, fraud, security breach, dependence on key personnel, and incorrect processing?

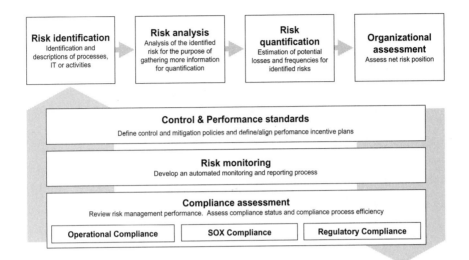

EXHIBIT 3.1 ENTERPRISE RISK MANAGEMENT CYCLE

Checklist: Risks to Identify

☐ System risk resulting from programming errors, model/methodology error, mark-to-market error, IT systems failure, telecommunication failure, deficient MIS, deficient contingency planning

☐ Reputation risk resulting from loss of confidential data, inability to conduct operations (disaster/critical system failure), clumsiness in conducting operations

☐ People risk arising from lack of integrity, competence, management/governance

☐ Regulatory risk arising from noncompliance with specific industry and/or externally imposed regulations and guidelines

Risk Analysis/Quantification

Checklist: Risk Analysis Questions to Consider

- ☐ Which risks are most likely to occur?
- ☐ Which would have the most impact on the organization's ability to achieve its objectives?
- ☐ What are the financial implications to the business if the risk occurs?
- ☐ What implications are there on the entity's reputation?
- ☐ What risks will the organization not accept (e.g., quality compromises)?
- ☐ What risks will the organization accept for new initiatives (e.g., new product lines)?
- ☐ What risks will the organization accept for competing objectives (e.g., gross profit versus market share)?

Checklist: Key Actions

- ☐ *Assess risk.* Risk assessment is the identification and analysis of events/occurrences that may prevent the achievement of business objectives. It forms a basis for determining how risks should be managed.
- ☐ *Determine risk appetite.* Risk appetite is the amount of broad-based risk an entity is willing to accept in pursuit of value. It can be expressed in quantitative or qualitative terms (e.g., earnings at risk vs. reputation risk) and should also include consideration of risk tolerance (range of acceptable variation).

Organizational Assessment

Having assessed relevant risk, management now determines how it will respond. In considering its response, management assesses the likelihood and potential impact as well as cost and benefits, selecting a response that brings residual risk within desired risk tolerances.

Checklist: Quantification of Risk Exposure

- [ ] Determine risk response among four major categories:
  1. Accept = monitor
  2. Avoid = eliminate (get out of situation)
  3. Reduce = institute controls
  4. Share = partner with someone (e.g., insurance)
- [ ] Residual risk (unmitigated risk)

Reporting and Monitoring

Communicate Results

The following are potential methods/tools utilized for the communication of risks and the results of the risk assessment:

- Dashboard of risks and related responses (visual status of where key risks stand relative to risk tolerances)

- Flowcharts of processes with key controls noted

- Narratives of business objectives linked to operational risks and responses

- List of key risks to be monitored

- Management understanding of key business risk responsibility and communication of assignments

Monitor

Checklist: Ongoing Risk Monitoring Process

- [ ] Collect and display information

☐ Perform analysis

☐ Management oversight and periodic review

    ◻ Definition of individual accountability and ownership for risks and risk mitigation

    ◻ Updates of ERM plan based on changes in business objectives, systems, and processes

RISK MANAGEMENT REQUIRES A WELL-INFORMED AUDIT COMMITTEE

The Sarbanes-Oxley Act has placed a spotlight on the audit committee and the increased responsibilities of members as guardians of corporate governance and investors' interests. In turn, the relationship between the audit committee and executive management (particularly the CEO and CFO) has changed as both groups assume increased responsibility for oversight of the financial reporting process, the assurance of the accuracy and transparency of financial statements, and risk management.

In order to provide effective oversight, the audit committee should expect management, particularly the CFO, to provide the information needed to help members expand their knowledge and awareness of the company's financial reporting process, including identifying risks and understanding the level of existence of controls surrounding those risks. Members do not need to be inundated with detail, but they should receive enough information to fully understand the company's compliance strategy and approach. Audit committee members should ensure that they have adequate information in order to make informed decisions. The CEO and CFO should expect the audit committee to reinforce the tone at the top as well as the expectations set by executive management for developing and maintaining strong financial controls and an environment of accurate financial reporting.

Full management support can result in a more effective and focused audit committee and lead to the identification of process efficiencies, more effective risk management, and ongoing compliance cost reduction. To attain such a level of effectiveness, the CFO should provide audit committee members with the necessary information/insight to appropriately answer the following questions:

1. **What are the company's risk management strategy, plan, and process? Does the plan include consideration of nonfinancial risks (e.g., operational, market, reputation)?** Organizations with a formal comprehensive risk management plan can proactively identify uncertainties and manage business risks by aligning their strategies, processes, people, and technology.

2. **Does the organization's risk management process appropriately identify and manage risks?** Companies that assess risks across all business activities can eliminate functional and business silos and speed risk identification, which gives management more time to determine whether to avoid it, reduce it, share it, or accept it.

3. **How is Sarbanes-Oxley compliance integrated into the overall risk management plan?** Company initiatives and overall compliance requirements can compete for internal resources and management attention. Developing a common framework that manages all regulatory requirements can provide considerable savings and efficiency.

4. **What are the top ten overall risks of the company? What are their potential impacts? What is the potential financial exposure?** Every organization should assess and document all risks and the overall impact of each and subsequently rank them accordingly.

5. **How does the risk management plan address the company's top ten overall risks? What is being done to mitigate them?** A detailed mitigation plan should be documented and

implemented for each of the highest-ranked risks. Mitigation plans should include action that optimally minimizes risk.

6. **If an ERM plan is already in place, does it focus on maximizing shareholder value?** Effective risk management plans help management assess future events and anticipate risks that can lead to value enhancement.

7. **What is the organization's risk tolerance? How is it determined?** Audit committee members should agree that the risk appetite of the organization is in proper balance with the company's strategic objectives and business needs.

8. **Have key risk indicators been identified? If so, how are they monitored?** Clearly defined key risk indicators are the foundation for achieving the full benefits of a formal risk management plan. Performance measures that are difficult to understand or not effectively monitored often lead to reduced effectiveness.

9. **Is the entire organization, not just senior management, aware of risk and educated on how it should be addressed?** A communication and/or education/training plan should be drafted and implemented in order to heighten the awareness and understanding of company risks and risk mitigation plans, policies, and procedures.

10. **What surprises have occurred in the past and what was done to address such events so they do not recur?** Once the audit committee is aware of past surprises, it should seek to understand if the company's risk profile and mitigation plans have changed as a result.

Regulations have placed greater demands and expectations on the audit committee, thereby requiring members to expand their awareness of the methods and participants in the organization's financial reporting and risk management process. The audit committee should expect the CFO to play an integral role in continually providing financial information and candid assessments of company performance, which can be used to monitor efficiencies, manage risks, and reduce costs.

MAXIMIZE FUTURE PERFORMANCE THROUGH BPM AND ERM INTEGRATION

The Sarbanes-Oxley Act forced a heightened focus on the financial risks within an organization. Many companies have limited their primary consideration to financial risks, thus adopting a narrow approach to risk management. Ignoring or minimizing operational risks when evaluating a company's performance and future prospects can leave management blindsided by events that erode shareholder value. In order to obtain a holistic, forward-looking, and accurate view of what events may impact the business and hinder the achievement of strategic goals, companies should adopt a more comprehensive outlook and integrate operational risks into their overall BPM strategy. Here are nine steps to effectively integrate BPM and ERM:

Nine Steps to Effectively Integrate BPM and ERM

Step 1. If you don't have one, establish an enterprise-wide risk management infrastructure.

Step 2. Develop a risk management reporting system that covers all levels of the organization, from the department/business unit level up through the entire enterprise.

Step 3. Determine which types of reports the executive committee and board will need and which should remain at the department/business unit level.

Step 4. Decide what information will be needed to effectively identify and evaluate risk. Determine if this data already exists or whether it needs to be captured.

Step 5. Examine BPM metrics and databases to see if there is any duplication with ERM metrics.

Step 6. Develop a conceptual report on an integrated BPM-ERM reporting system that covers all levels.

Step 7. Determine if the organization has the skill sets and availability to develop an integrated reporting system in-house or whether outside assistance will be needed.

Step 8. Ensure that appropriate management processes (e.g., individual, divisional) are in place to reinforce the integrated BPM-ERM approach within the company culture.

Step 9. Engage senior executives, particularly the CEO, in the process because their sponsorship is essential to success.

Integration Captures Past, Present, and Future Performance

The Committee of Sponsoring Organizations of the Treadway Commission (COSO) recommends that organizations proactively manage risks by implementing ERM—practices that identify potential events that could affect the organization and manage the risks associated with such events—across the enterprise to provide reasonable assurance that company objectives will be met. A comprehensive approach to risk management can strengthen a company's BPM efforts by preparing it for events that traditional financial forecasting and planning processes would miss. BPM focuses primarily on performance monitoring to ensure that business objectives at various levels of the organization have been achieved with minimal variance from plan, so many of the key performance indicators (KPIs) captured in management reports reflect only historical performance data.

ERM, in contrast, evaluates the risk profile of the company across all of its departments and lines of business. The key risk indicators (KRIs) that ERM processes generate are predictive indicators of future performance. Therefore, an organization that uses a combined BPM and ERM system to support management decision making is basing decisions on a complete picture that includes past, present, and future performance. Looking at a company's KPIs without fully understanding the risk environment in which it operates can leave management open to surprises that can rapidly dominate the organization.

The Benefits of a Joint Approach

Companies that employ both BPM and ERM frequently inherently disconnect the two, especially at the senior executive and board levels. United, the two processes can provide several compelling benefits: (1) because managing business risk is integral to managing business performance, companies that include risk assessments in their financial planning and forecasting can develop a realistic expectation of their future performance and clearly see the environmental factors that are most likely to affect their profitability; and (2) proactive management of performance and the creation of shareholder value are possible only when BPM and ERM are fully integrated with a company's routine management activities and daily operations. When performed separately from BPM, ERM remains an add-on that is frequently not well executed.

Fortunately, joint ERM and BPM projects are more practical today than ever before by using more affordable and user-friendly technology. Historically, one of the biggest obstacles to combining these activities has been the consolidation of all necessary information from disparate software platforms, locations, and business units. In the past few years, the Internet and the XML data markup language have become increasingly popular gateways for information exchange. Some software vendors now provide extract, transform, and load data capabilities through XML protocols, which facilitate data management and eliminate the need for costly interfaces to pull information from multiple platforms into a single application. In addition, sophisticated new data management applications can bring information together from a variety of databases and multiple platforms to give end users a single view of the enterprise.

4

ADDRESSING COMPLIANCE CHALLENGES THROUGH AUTOMATION

Organizations invested millions of dollars in initial compliance, and subsequently spent as much as 80 percent of those same dollars in year two refining documentation, testing, and remediating control weaknesses. Now, as they move through year three and beyond, companies are exploring automation as a means for making the ongoing compliance process more efficient and less costly.

As a result of several factors, not the least of which being a lack of integrated testing as well as a significant amount of manual compliance testing and reporting, external audit costs have also increased—in many cases, significantly. Lack of automation has also contributed to the high cost of compliance. In many organizations, a high number of manual controls still remain, and a substantial amount of manual testing continues to occur.

Compliance monitoring, testing, and reporting automation can play a key role in achieving process improvement and efficiency. When implemented effectively, technology enables an efficient, repeatable, and reliable process that can significantly lower the cost of compliance and offer increased visibility into the business. It can also strengthen the control environment, increase data integrity, improve process efficiency, and minimize risk by providing better visibility into control issues, allowing organizations to address known concerns earlier and avoid misstatements or certification issues.

The reasons most often cited for not implementing technology are a lack of time, resources, and expertise. Companies typically utilized existing systems and processes to meet stringent compliance deadlines during year one and two of compliance. Most did not have the capabilities to identify, evaluate, and implement technology as part of their initial compliance efforts. Other organizations delayed automation until they could determine how SOX compliance will integrate into their overall long-term business strategies. Still others chose to wait until the software market and available tools were more mature and sophisticated.

These reasons for delaying automation are no longer valid in the current regulatory environment, where 100 percent accuracy and integrity in financial reporting are expected. In order to address the demand for an efficient, cost-effective method of compliance, senior finance executives are elevating the importance of automation within their organizations.

According to an August 2005 study conducted by CFO Research Services, more than 75 percent of the top finance executives surveyed assigned either "top priority" or "moderate priority" (versus "low priority" or an "I don't know" response) to the automation of their compliance and control environment over the next 12 months. These executives justifiably expect automation to provide a complete and accurate view of the controls, which in turn will create a higher level of confidence in senior management's ability to monitor and direct compliance efforts.

Year three of compliance is an ideal time for a company to consider implementing a tool that facilitates the execution of its strategy. The current software market offers a comprehensive array of tools that support the automation of the compliance management, monitoring, and reporting processes. These tools can also effectively integrate SOX compliance with related areas such as internal audit, enterprise risk management, and additional regulatory requirements. While much work remains for companies to achieve an optimal framework for sustainable compliance, automation plays a vital role in providing that framework and significantly reducing both short-term and long-term costs.

Numerous companies face the challenge of documenting controls across multiple locations and disparate accounting systems. According to a recent study, the average $1 billion company maintains 48 financial programs along with nearly three enterprise resource planning (ERP) systems. Such challenges have enticed more than 80 vendors to develop various software solutions aimed at Section 404 compliance. The list includes ERP vendors, content management and business-process management specialists, startups, and industry giants. With so many choices available, determining which product to implement is not an easy decision. As a result, software selection projects are becoming a necessary means for reaching a consensus on what tool should be used to facilitate ongoing SOX compliance.

SOFTWARE CAN ADD VALUE BEYOND COMPLIANCE

Most public companies would agree that Section 404 of the Sarbanes-Oxley Act (SOX) and its resultant reporting deadlines have made manual documentation and control testing increasingly difficult. The need to demonstrate sound financial controls over key business processes and test those controls annually has led many organizations down the path of automation.

The benefits of technology are certainly compelling. SOX-specific software can provide clear evidence that internal controls are in place and operating effectively, which can give executive management added confidence when certifying the effectiveness of controls. Perhaps even more important is technology's ability to improve ongoing compliance efforts (and alleviate staff frustration) by streamlining documentation and facilitating continuous improvement. Before employing automation, organizations should seek to first incorporate a compliance mindset into their culture. A compliance software implementation coupled with the rollout of a complete ongoing compliance process can help facilitate this integration, so that compliance ultimately becomes another business process that is woven into the culture of the organization.

Implementing compliance software offered by one of the leading providers can help companies improve their compliance as well as business processes. Such products provide distinctive capabilities in compliance monitoring, maintenance, and reporting automation and offer unique features and benefits beyond just compliance management. Certain tools identify and score enterprise-wide risks based on significance and likelihood of occurrence and measure variance from targeted risk standards. Other software applications unify financial reporting and close tasks with internal controls, thereby increasing the precision and timeliness of financial statements and reducing the risk of material weakness disclosures. Overall, these tools can add significant value above and beyond compliance management when tailored to a company's individual requirements.

Monitoring Software

Automation, specifically the use of continuous monitoring, can facilitate ongoing compliance goals such as reducing costs, strengthening the control environment, increasing data integrity, minimizing risk, and improving business processes. Real-time transaction inspection and reporting software can assist with strengthening the control environment, sustaining SOX compliance, reducing ongoing compliance costs, minimizing risk, and potentially deliver a return on investment.

In addition, continuous monitoring of financial processes and real-time transaction inspection and reporting software can sustain

SOX compliance and potentially deliver a return on investment by continuously monitoring financial processes, automating manual controls, and facilitating process improvement. Serving as an automated audit, transaction integrity monitoring software can be instrumental in performing the following:

- Monitoring the effectiveness of preventive controls

- Asserting the compliance of individual transactions

- Identifying exceptions before they become control deficiencies

- Alerting compliance officers to control violations

Errors in day-to-day financial transactions consistently result in adjustments, reversals, and rework. Continuous monitoring drives defect-free financial processes to eliminate potential weaknesses in the control environment by inspecting each step of every financial transaction in real time for errors and control violations, thus eliminating associated costs. Increasing the quality of financial operations leads to an accelerated, more accurate close process and validates policy compliance. Monitoring software inspects each step of every financial transaction in real time for errors and control violations. This allows an organization to immediately, proactively address any identified issues, while minimizing the associated cost of correction. In addition, automated controls and the implementation of real-time transaction inspection deliver results that give executive management the confidence to sign the Section 302 and 404 certifications.

Monitoring software vendors have elevated continuous controls monitoring to the next level by combining controls testing with real-time transaction inspection to identify the problems in a business process. Their platform automates the entire life cycle of finding problems, fixing them, and proving they were effectively resolved. By inspecting each step of individual transactions across systems, this automated process identifies all errors and control violations, drives defect-free processes, and sustains SOX compliance in a cost-effective manner. Many organizations have expanded the use of monitoring tools beyond compliance and have recognized a significant return on investment.

In addition to assisting in sustaining SOX compliance, real-time transaction inspection can transform compliance expense into a return on compliance investment. Transaction integrity monitoring serves as an automated audit.

In addition, it minimizes control testing, streamlines the monitoring and reporting process, and, most important, provides a cost-effective ongoing compliance process.

Utilization of Continuous Monitoring: Control Testing and Control Automation

Use of continuous monitoring for control testing involves monitoring a control that is already in place (defined and performed within the existing process). In this case, the monitoring for control breakdowns has been automated. In other words, a control exists and activity is being monitored to identify exceptions or control violations. Subsequently, those specific incidents/instances are addressed and/or corrected. An example would be monitoring journal entry approval for exceptions such as approval by the preparer.

Use of continuous monitoring for control automation involves removing manual activity from the procedure by replacing manual control with an automated process that contains the control. An example would be monitoring for duplicate vendor payments. Continuous monitoring can serve many purposes. Many organizations have successfully employed continuous monitoring for control testing and control automation, which has resulted in ongoing compliance cost reduction via a reduction in testing.

Use of technology for these purposes has been reinforced by the regulatory agencies. The SEC guidance provided in the May 2005 and 2006 Releases supports this type of automation. Both Releases reinforced a risk-based approach and, more importantly for this discussion, automated application controls and testing. In the May 2005 Release, the SEC stated the following regarding automated application controls:

> Auditors may conclude that automated application control continues to be effective, without repeating the prior year testing of the application if:
>
> -General controls over program changes, access to programs, and computer operations are effective and continue to be tested <u>AND</u>
>
> -The auditor verifies that the automated application control has not changed since he or she last tested the application control

The key message in this statement is a resultant reduction in testing, thus a reduction in cost, driven by automation, more specifically continuous monitoring.

Benefits of Continuous Monitoring

Several benefits can be derived from both automated control testing and control automation through continuous monitoring. Primarily, it reduces cost by reducing the compliance control testing effort required. It inherently strengthens the control environment and minimizes risk resulting from the increase in preventive control and the reduction in manual processing/human intervention. Elimination of manual activity minimizes risk. Continuous monitoring applications provide a detailed audit trail and automated status reporting. Both of these functions facilitate an efficient external audit through a reduction in the amount of internal and auditor resource time spent on preparation and review of information.

In addition, automated control testing and control automation can facilitate overall process improvement, which can lead to cost reduction and allow for a focus on more value-added activity. Many organizations have been utilizing external resources for compliance testing. A reduction in manual testing and an increase in control automation can lead to a decrease in the use of external resources, which, in turn, results in cost reduction.

Continuous Monitoring Tool Considerations

In evaluating continuous monitoring tools, the following functions should be considered:

Functions to Consider When Evaluating Continuous Monitoring Tools

☐ **Monitoring beyond just the ERP application.** An organization should seek to have the ability to access all source systems. This provides a comprehensive data set for an independent analysis versus the qualified assertions existent in exclusive ERP monitoring.

☐ **Single-exception identification.** In other words, a monitoring system that only identifies an exception one time. For example, if an application is being monitored and reported on daily and an exception is documented today, this same exception should not show on the exception log again tomorrow with newly identified exceptions. This duplicate reporting would warrant reconciliation, which requires resource time and attention and increases cost.

☐ **False-positive minimization.** Certainly there is a cost to implementing a continuous monitoring system and a cost to handling identified exceptions. The goal is to minimize false positives that require time and money to address.

A continuous monitoring application should provide a unified view of process integrity that includes not only compliance considerations but also the entire business process. This can lead to overall business process improvement and cost reduction.

THE CONTINUOUS MONITORING PROCESS

The continuous monitoring process, at its very simplest, requires data acquisition, storage/warehousing, and analysis, as well as definition of a violation remediation process.

Data Acquisition

The data and transaction acquisition process facilitates data gathering from multiple disparate systems/applications. It allows for implementation of batch data extractions on a periodic basis (e.g., daily, weekly) based on any partial/changed data according to a defined "data changed" field. This method of extraction normalizes and standardizes data across applications and therefore creates a universal transaction flow. If real-time extractions are performed based on algorithms, the process can be executed without impacting or interrupting application performance.

Data Warehousing

Subsequent to data extraction, a read-only copy of detailed data can be stored, and a complete archived history of all data becomes a permanent record in a compliance monitoring vault. This storage process operates independently of all source systems, and data snapshots are maintained for specific moments in time and states of the business. Therefore, transaction streams can be replayed for retrospective inspection and analysis.

Data Analysis

Inspection of stored data facilitates the identification of data concerns such as internal control issues and segregation of duties. In addition, data comparisons can be executed that identify exact duplicates and/or transactions that exceed specified thresholds. Customized rules can be utilized to report yes/no conditions and signal alerts based on dollar-value thresholds.

Intelligent reasoning can be applied to the analysis process, and transactions within a network of related documents, processes, and actions can be reviewed for the following considerations:

- Multisystem segregation of duties

- Process level out-of-sequence events, which may be an indication of collusion

- Real-time, risk-based analysis

- Usage abuse and/or privileged user abuse, which may be an indication of collusion

- Identification of errors of omission

Exception Remediation

The final step in the continuous monitoring process offers a violation resolution method that is automated from start to finish. Proof of remediation and compliance is provided.

Identified violations are addressed as follows:

- Actionable alerts are communicated via e-mail to designated individuals.

- Prioritization and escalation is based on predetermined thresholds or conditions, and issues are escalated through the proper resolution channel.

- Issues are identified and addressed prior to the close and reporting in order to avoid problems during the month-end process.

- Corrections are detected and performed.

A long-term compliance plan that includes implementation of technology that performs continuous monitoring for the purposes of control monitoring and/or control testing can effectively minimize cost, strengthen the control environment, facilitate accurate financial reporting and disclosure, and improve processes.

RISK MANAGEMENT SOFTWARE

A lack of standardized, automated, and integrated processes can lead to inefficiency and increased cost. In addition, it can hinder an organization's ability to make informed and accurate decisions about enterprise risk management.

Every organization can benefit from taking a holistic view of risk in relation to its long- and short-term strategic goals. Risk management software facilitates this process by helping executives, risk managers, and process owners effectively analyze all relevant risks impacting their organizations. These platforms integrate SOX compliance, general compliance, internal audit, and risk management through a central data repository that produces more accurate information and promotes the consistency of internal controls.

Several standard reports and reporting features exist within this type of solution (e.g., dashboards and scorecards) that outline and categorize the risks that can impact the business. Extensive ad hoc reporting capabilities are also available that can produce customized reports without relying on IT support. Such a solution can later be expanded into a comprehensive risk management module that provides a detailed view of all identified material and relevant risks in order to reduce deficiencies in internal controls, streamline business processes, and implement a proactive approach to risk management.

Utilizing technology to build and monitor an ERM program can help an organization:

- Continuously monitor risks and controls

- Integrate and link risks and controls

- Track remediation

- Integrate audit and assurance activity

- Disseminate risk assessment information throughout the organization

Overall, risk management software improves business integrity by ensuring the accuracy of information and internal controls. Perhaps even more important is the software's ability, in many cases, to eliminate the need for multiple technology solutions, thereby dramatically reducing the time, resources, and costs associated with compliance, risk management, and audit initiatives.

UNIFYING FINANCIAL STATEMENTS, CLOSE TASKS, AND SOX CONTROLS

Experts estimate that most senior financial executives believe their current processes and systems are insufficient to deliver sustained, cost-effective compliance with the Sarbanes-Oxley Act. A recent analysis conducted by software company Movaris substantiates this thinking. The study revealed that 31 percent of companies with material weakness disclosures had weaknesses in operational finance, with 46 percent of those relating to the close and consolidation process.[1]

Most companies complete their SOX assessment after their financial close, which can delay the detection of failed key controls. Discovering failed controls after the financial close requires the reevaluation of financial results and may lead to materials weakness disclosures and financial restatements. This can be an expensive, time-consuming, and risky process in today's environment of

---

1. Movaris analysis of publicly filed MWDs for 2004.

increasingly complex accounting rules and regulatory requirements. Since the passing of the Act in 2002, restatements have
grown from 330 to an astounding estimated 1,200 in 2005.[2] This
finding reinforces the fact that improvements must be made to
strengthen controls and efficiently obtain an accurate assessment of
a company's financial position.

There is an inherent risk in continuing to rely on manual and/or
disparate processes for financial reporting and compliance. Regulatory guidance instructs companies to integrate the SOX review of
internal controls with the periodic preparation and audit of financial statements, yet the ability to do so has eluded most companies
until the recent arrival of sophisticated software tools. Some of
these tools directly link financial controls and close tasks to a company's financial statements, creating a system of record for both
financial close and financial compliance. Streamlining and automating manual financial close and compliance processes allows
CFOs to minimize one of their largest expenses—external auditor
fees.

Every organization should seek to automate the financial close
process and link financial controls to financial statements. This
minimizes the risk of material weakness disclosure and financial
restatement, as well as increases the accuracy and auditability of
financial statements.

Determining the Right Solution

When selecting a software solution, an organization should first
consider its overall short- and long-term strategies and evaluate how
each software option will facilitate the achievement of those goals. In
addition, the company should determine what compliance activities
it would like to automate. Specific high-level application functionality requirements may include some or all of the following:

---

2. "Restatements – Traversing Shaky Ground," Glass Lewis & Co, January
2006.

- Document management

- Control testing/assessment/certification automation

- Monitoring management

- Risk management

Consider the following methodology when determining which software is most appropriate for support of the ongoing compliance process:

Define Business Requirements

An analysis of the current and anticipated activities that would be required to comply with SOX legislation should be conducted. This analysis will help establish a point of reference for assessing the benefits of implementing a software tool to reduce the costs of compliance and more effectively manage the compliance process.

Checklist: Tasks to Define Business Requirements

- ☐ Develop an estimate of the activities associated with compliance, including the number of documented processes, total number of documents to be stored and maintained, controls activities to be monitored, and estimated annual employee hours dedicated to compliance.

- ☐ Document any existing issues with the current compliance process, such as document management and version control, scheduling of control evaluations/tests, data integrity, control testing, and status reporting.

- ☑ Conduct interviews with senior managers in departments such as Internal Audit, Financial Reporting, and Operational Management to obtain input regarding requirements and existing challenges.

☐ Prepare and prioritize a list of functionality, technical preferences, and desired vendor characteristics from the results of the interviews.

Identify Vendor Candidates

A significant number of software options are currently available. These tools range from expensive, robust solutions that fully integrate many components of SOX compliance to inexpensive, free-standing solutions that are not specifically designed for SOX, but are well suited to address particular aspects of compliance such as document management. From this extensive list, candidates that meet the documented business requirements should be contacted for initial discussions and potential product demonstrations.

Select Tool and Plan Implementation

After performing product demonstrations and providing an initial investment quote and product information, the software vendors should be scored based on their ability to meet the documented requirements. Scores and analysis should be weighed, and the following factors should be strongly considered when making a final vendor decision:

- The technical requirements of the software and its alignment with organizational and IT strategy

- Software flexibility and expansion of use based on long-term organizational goals

- Remarks offered by references

- Application user-friendliness (ease of design and use)

- Implementation requirements (e.g., time, resources, cost)

- Cost

Once the vendor is selected, implementation planning can begin.

For many companies, the benefits of automation greatly outweigh the upfront investment when coupled with the risk of non-compliance. Technology itself is not the ticket to hard cost savings (a common misconception), but an investment that facilitates change and helps the company remain dynamic in an environment inhibited by increased corporate governance and the costly burden of compliance.

A

Ongoing Compliance Checklist

PLAN, DESIGN, AND BUILD

- ☐ Appoint compliance owner(s)
- ☐ Define roles and responsibilities
- ☐ Define role of internal audit
- ☐ Define reporting relationships
- ☐ Develop skill profiles and requirements
  - ☐ Prepare and/or update job descriptions
- ☐ Perform skill assessment
  - ☐ Identify resource gaps
- ☐ Develop resource plan
- ☐ Design and develop communication and training plan
- ☐ Determine reporting requirements
- ☐ Design reporting process
- ☐ Develop testing strategy and review plans
- ☐ Design monitoring process
- ☐ Determine technology options and requirements
- ☐ Define key performance measurements
- ☐ Draft initial implementation plan

- [ ] Develop and present recommendations and preliminary project plan
- [ ] Validate design with stakeholders
- [ ] Refine initial plan based on constituents' input and all of the above

IMPLEMENT

- [ ] Assign roles and responsibilities
- [ ] Implement resource plan
- [ ] Review and/or write compliance policies
- [ ] Execute communication plan
- [ ] Conduct plan kickoff and rollout
- [ ] Deliver training
- [ ] Build reporting package
- [ ] Develop program management tools
- [ ] Perform control testing
- [ ] Obtain testing signoff
- [ ] Implement monitoring process
- [ ] Process/control changes
- [ ] Identify remediation issues
- [ ] Key performance measurements
- [ ] Install enabling technology
- [ ] Load data into enabling technology
- [ ] Populate reports

INDEX